Hans Holbein

by

Arthur B. Chamberlain

Double 9 BOOKS

Hans Holbein
by Arthur B. Chamberlain

ISBN: 978-93-62200-83-9

Published by

DOUBLE 9 BOOKS

2/13-B, Ansari Road
Daryaganj, New Delhi – 110002
info@double9books.com
www.double9books.com
Tel. 011-40042856

ABOUT THE AUTHOR

Arthur B. Chamberlain, a distinguished author of his time, is celebrated for his magnum opus, "Hans Holbein." This seminal work stands as a testament to Chamberlain's unparalleled expertise in art history and his profound understanding of the human spirit. Through meticulous research and evocative prose, Chamberlain brings to life the illustrious painter Hans Holbein, illuminating the complexities of his art and the tumultuous times in which he lived. In "Hans Holbein," Chamberlain delves into the life and work of the renowned Renaissance artist, offering readers a comprehensive exploration of his genius and legacy. With keen insight and scholarly rigor, Chamberlain unravels the mysteries behind Holbein's masterpieces, shedding light on the artist's techniques, inspirations, and enduring impact on the world of art. Through vivid descriptions and compelling narratives, Chamberlain transports readers to the vibrant streets of Renaissance Europe, where art and culture flourished amidst political intrigue and religious upheaval. "Hans Holbein" is more than just a biography; it is a captivating journey through the corridors of history, where Chamberlain's passion for his subject shines through on every page. This groundbreaking work cements Chamberlain's legacy as a preeminent scholar and author, leaving an indelible mark on the world of art history.

CONTENTS

LIFE OF HANS HOLBEIN

EARLY DAYS IN AUGSBURG AND BASLE

HANS HOLBEIN was born, in 1497, at Augsburg, in Swabia, Southern Germany, to which town his grandfather, Michael Holbein, had moved, some time before 1454, from the neighbouring village of Schönenfeld. His father, known to-day as Holbein the elder, to distinguish him from his more celebrated son, was one of the leading painters of Augsburg, and an artist of importance in the history of German art.

The elder Holbein was one of the first of German painters strongly influenced by the Italian Renaissance, and a chronological study of his pictures shows very clearly how great a change was gradually taking place north of the Alps both in artistic ideals and technical methods, through an increasing knowledge of what the great painters of the Southern peninsula had accomplished. In his early work he shows himself to be a follower of Rogier van der Weyden and his school, but towards the end of the first decade of the sixteenth century the Gothic qualities of his painting, with its many hardnesses and angularities, begin to disappear, and a closer observation and a more truthful rendering of nature to take their place. He threw off one by one his Rhenish traditions, and replaced them by the methods of the Van Eycks, which reached him indirectly through the mellowing influence of the earlier Venetian painters. He developed, too, a fondness for rich architectural decoration of the Renaissance type for the backgrounds and settings of his pictures, in the use of which his son, later on, became so perfect a master.

As a result of certain forged documents and false inscriptions, a number of interesting works, formerly ascribed rightly to the father, were taken from him and given to the son, and hailed as signs of precocious genius. Even the father's masterpiece, *The Martyrdom of St. Sebastian* at Munich, did not escape the enthusiasm of the younger artist's biographers. Modern criticism, however, has restored to the father a series of works which place him among the leading painters of Germany at the dawn of the new movement in art.

Hans Holbein the younger seems to have received no artistic training except that which he gained in his father's studio or workshop, where his elder brother Ambrosius was also engaged. His uncle Sigismund, too, was an Augsburg painter, and may have helped in his instruction. His father, though constantly in debt and difficulties, seems to have received numerous orders for altar-pieces and other sacred pictures, so that the workshop was a busy one, and no doubt young Hans began at an early age to help in such minor details as the painting of draperies and backgrounds. Much of his genius was inherited from his father, particularly that remarkable power of portraying character with a few vivid strokes of the pencil which is one of the crowning glories of his art.

In those days a young painter generally finished his education by a year or two of travel before settling down as a master painter in the guild of his native town. Ambrose and Hans Holbein seem to have followed the prevailing fashion, leaving Augsburg towards the end of 1514 or early in 1515. In the latter year the father went to Issenheim in High Alsace to paint an altar-piece, and the two young men may have gone with him. There is some probability, too, that the whole family settled in Lucerne about this time. In any case, the two sons were residing in Basle before the end of 1515, any plan of extended travel being cut short by the prospect of plenty of work. At that time Basle was the northern centre of the great revival of literature and learning, and several of its printers were of European reputation. Many of the chief works of the leading humanist writers were first published in Basle, and decorated with woodcut illustrations and ornamental title-pages and borders. The prospect of employment upon "black-and-white" work of this kind was, no doubt, one of the chief attractions which brought the two young painters to the town. Nor were they disappointed, for shortly after their arrival a commission was given to them by Johann Froben, Erasmus's publisher, and the principal printer of the city.

It is not unlikely that the young men first of all entered the workshop of some Basle painter, such as that of Hans Herbster, whose portrait was painted in 1516 by one of the two brothers. Until recently this picture was in the collection of the Earl of Northbrook, and ascribed to Hans, but since its acquisition by the Basle Museum it has been attributed to Ambrose. The latter, of whose work we know very little, seems to have been an artist of only moderate capabilities. He joined the Painters' Guild in Basle in 1517, and, as no record of him has been found later than 1519, he is supposed to have died young.

During the next seven or eight years Holbein designed a number of book illustrations for Froben, Adam Petri, Thomas Wolff, and other printers. He was ready, however, to turn his hand to anything. He painted a table with an amusing allegory of St. Nobody for the wedding of Hans Bär in Basle on June 24, 1515, and in the same year supplied a schoolmaster with a sign-board to hang outside his house.

It is uncertain when Holbein first became acquainted with the great scholar of Antwerp, Desiderius Erasmus, who had come to Basle in 1513 for the purpose of superintending the publishing of his books, nor is it easy to say to what degree of intimacy the artist was admitted by this brilliant humanist. Erasmus had the greatest admiration for his powers as an artist, and served him whenever he could, both by employing him himself and recommending him to others. During Holbein's first year in Basle, Erasmus had published through Froben his famous and witty satire, "The Praise of Folly," and the artist made a number of drawings on the margins of a copy of this book, illustrating passages in the text. He seems to have done them at the suggestion of another distinguished man of letters, Oswald Molitor, of Lucerne, at that time employed by Froben, who selected the passages to be illustrated; and a note in his handwriting says that they were finished on December 29, 1515, and that Erasmus was greatly entertained by them. The original book is now in the Basle Museum.

Holbein soon began to give proof of his wonderful abilities as a portrait painter. One of the first commissions he received was in 1516, from Jacob Meyer, Burgomaster of Basle, whom he painted, together with his young second wife, Dorothea Kannegiesser, a double portrait in one frame (Basle Museum). The burgomaster was pleased with the result, and remained the artist's constant good friend, procuring important public commissions for him, as well as making further private use of his talents.

In 1517 he left Basle for Lucerne, where, according to Dr. von Liebenau, his father was then residing. He was made a member of the recently-founded Painters' Guild of St. Luke, and also joined a local company of archers. On December 10, 1517, he was in trouble with the magistrates, being fined for taking part in some street brawl, after which he appears to have left Lucerne for a time. He can be traced as far south as Altdorf by the remains of a few pictures. If he ever visited Italy it would be at this period. One or two writers hold that he made some such journey, and point to several paintings in the Basle Museum as proof that he must have had personal acquaintance with certain achievements of Leonardo and his school, which he could only have seen in Italy; but the influence of Mantegna and Da Vinci, which, though plainly detected in his early work, is by no means a predominant one, may be easily accounted for through the numerous Italian engravings then circulating throughout Europe, without any actual visit to Lombardy on the part of the artist. He was back in Lucerne in 1518, busily engaged upon the decoration of the house of the magistrate, Jacob von Hertenstein, which he covered with frescoes both inside and out. The remains of this great work were destroyed in 1824, when the house was demolished for street improvements, but not before the chief designs had been hastily copied by Schwegher, Ulrich von Eschenbach, and other Lucerne artists. This was by far the most important undertaking upon which Holbein had as yet been engaged, and it was the first of a splendid series of decorative works of which, unhappily, nothing remains but their fame and a few slight preliminary sketches or indifferent copies. No one north of the Alps came near to him in the fertility of design and beauty of execution and of colour displayed by him in this adaptation of a favourite method of Italian decoration which became popular in the sixteenth century in certain parts of Germany and Switzerland.

Holbein was back in Basle in 1519. He joined the Painters' Guild on September 25, and on July 3 in the following year paid his fees as a burgher of the city. One of the first portraits he now undertook was that of *Bonifacius Amerbach*, a brilliant young scholar and intimate friend of Erasmus and other learned men. Amerbach had the greatest admiration for Holbein's genius, and missed no occasion of acquiring any of his works, and it is owing to his taste and liberal purse that so fine a collection of the painter's productions can be studied to-day in the Basle Museum.

The fame of Hertenstein's painted house had spread to Basle, and Holbein was soon busy over similar undertakings in the town of his adoption, of which the most celebrated was *The House of the Dance*. He also produced many designs for stained-glass windows, as well as a number of sketches for costumes and patterns for goldsmiths and metal-workers. His most important commission at this time, however, was the decoration of the interior of the new Town Hall with wall-paintings, showing that, although only twenty-four, he was already considered to be the chief artist in Basle. He began this work in June, 1521, and by November, 1522, had covered three of the walls with subjects taken from ancient history. These were probably selected for him, and were intended as examples of that exercise of stern justice which should characterize the actions and decisions of all rulers. These great decorative paintings have long since perished through damp and neglect, and only a few fragments remain in the Basle Museum. When he had finished three of the walls, he was of opinion that he had earned the full amount voted by the Town Council for the completion of the whole chamber. The Council saw the justice of this, but, cautious of their expenditure of the public funds, like many Councils of the present day, they resolved to "let the back wall alone until further notice."

In spite of these large decorative undertakings, Holbein found time to paint a number of sacred pictures, among the earlier ones being a *Passion* series, coarsely and hastily painted on canvas; a *Last Supper*, reminding one of more famous examples by Leonardo and Luini; and others which are described later on. His two greatest sacred pictures, which are worthy to stand by the side of the finest canvases of the Italians, are the *Madonna and Saints*, at Solothurn, painted in 1522, and the famous *Meyer Madonna*, at Darmstadt, (*see illustration*). The latter was executed about 1526 for the former burgomaster, Jacob Meyer.

Among other works of this period of the artist's career are two small portraits (Basle Museum), representing a certain Dorothea Offenburg, a lady of no great repute in her day, as *Venus with Cupid*, and again as *Lais Corinthiaca*. These are two of the pictures to which certain critics point as showing so strongly the influence of the Milanese school as to suggest a personal visit to Italy.

Holbein's fame as an illustrator largely depends upon his celebrated *Dance of Death* woodcuts, and his illustrations to the New Testament. Both series were commissioned by the brothers Trechsel, printers, of Lyons, about 1523, the designs from the pen of Holbein, and the blocks cut by Hans Lützelburger, the one engraver of the period who was fitted to reproduce Holbein's work in its full delicacy and beauty. Both artist and woodcutter seem to have been occupied with the commission until 1526, in which year Lützelburger died, and although Holbein had completed his part, the work stopped short for want of a competent engraver. Neither series was published until 1538, when Holbein was at his zenith as a portrait painter in England. *The Dance of Death* has been popularized by many reprints and reproductions; indeed, these satires on the uncertainty of life, homilies in miniature, drawn with the most surprising power and artistic beauty within the smallest limits, soon became famous throughout Europe.

FIRST VISIT TO ENGLAND

The Reformation in Switzerland, with the violent passions it aroused, made painting a precarious means of livelihood. Theological disputes agitated Basle from end to end, and the lower classes of the community were given over to disorder and discontent. Disturbances were of continual occurrence, culminating in the so-called Peasants' War. Privilege after privilege was wrested from the nobility and the great churchmen, and very many of the pictures, images, and decorations in the churches were wrecked by the fury of the mob in the fight for religious freedom. The Town Council was no longer in a position to encourage the development of the fine arts, and the Basle painters had a very hard struggle to live, and were glad of trivial employment, which in better times they would have scorned. Holbein, too, had married, about 1520, Elsbeth Schmidt, the widow of a tanner with one son, and had a young family of his own, so that he found it increasingly difficult to make both ends meet. He therefore thought seriously of visiting England in quest of work, probably at the suggestion of Erasmus, who had many friends and correspondents there. Holbein had painted his portrait more than once. One of the finest of them, sent by the learned humanist to Sir Thomas More, was probably the one now in Longford Castle (*see illustration*), dated 1523. A second example is the fine profile now in the Louvre. Erasmus wrote to Sir Thomas More about the artist, and More, in his reply, promised to do what he could for him when he came.

Holbein left Basle towards the end of August, 1526, and journeyed to England by way of Antwerp, where in all probability he made a short stay, reaching London about November. He was received with much kindness by Sir Thomas More, then Speaker of the House of Commons, and holding other high offices; and, according to tradition, remained as More's guest at his country house at Chelsea during the whole time of his first English visit. He seems to have confined his practice as a portrait painter entirely to Sir Thomas More's family and his immediate circle of friends, which was a large and learned one, embracing many of the leading churchmen, statesmen, and scholars of the day. More does not appear to have made him known to the King, although it is probable that Henry, who frequently visited the Speaker at Chelsea, and was a great patron of the fine arts, must have become acquainted, even as early as this, with Holbein's work.

In 1527 he painted Sir Thomas's portrait, the picture now in the possession of Mr. Edward Huth. In the same year he painted *William Wareham*, Archbishop of Canterbury. Two examples of this portrait exist, both by Holbein, at Lambeth Palace and in the Louvre, and two fine drawings, in the British Museum and at Windsor. Other portraits of 1527 are those of *Sir Henry Guildford*, the Lord Chamberlain (Windsor); his wife, *Lady Guildford* (Mr. Frewen's collection); *Sir Brian Tuke* (Munich and the Duke of Westminster); *John Fisher*, Bishop of Rochester, whose finished portrait is lost, but for which two fine sketches still exist (Windsor and the British Museum); and several undated works, such as the portrait of *Sir Henry Wyatt* (Louvre), were probably painted in this year. In 1528 he produced the fine portrait of *Nicholas Kratzer*, the King's Astronomer (Louvre), and *Thomas and John Godsalve*, of Norwich, on one panel (Dresden).

The most important work which he undertook at this time has, unfortunately, disappeared. This was the large portrait group of *Sir Thomas More and His Family*. Several versions of it still exist, of which the one at Nostell Priory is the most important, but not one of them is a genuine work of Holbein's. Happily, the very beautiful sketch for the whole composition is to-day one of the chief treasures of the Basle Museum. It was taken to Switzerland by the artist as a present from Sir Thomas to Erasmus. Several fine studies for the heads of the sitters have also been preserved (Windsor collection).

Mention must be made of another important undertaking with which there is good reason to believe that Holbein had much to do. Early in 1527 French Ambassadors were in London negotiating for an alliance between England and France. The signing of this treaty was celebrated at Greenwich on May 5, with much ceremonious festivity, concluding with a supper in a specially built banqueting-house. One of the chief painters engaged in the internal decoration of this building was a certain "Master Hans," a title by which Holbein was well known; and, common as this Christian name was in Germany, no trace has ever yet been found of any other artist named Hans then working in England except Holbein. The official direction of the building and decorating of this temporary hall was in the hands of Sir Henry Guildford, and it would be natural for him to turn to the craftsman of whose artistic powers he had full knowledge. It was the kind of work, too, for which Holbein was already celebrated in Switzerland. He appears to have been appointed to supervise the numerous painters employed, and frequent mention is made of "Master Hans and his company" (Calendar of State Papers, 1526-1528). By March 2 "Master Hans" had left Greenwich, and was busily engaged in London upon a large "plat," or picture, of *The Battle of Spurs*. He had finished this in a month, and was paid £4 10s. for it. This picture was fixed on the back of an arch which divided the banqueting-hall from the gallery leading to the ball-room. Considering the occasion for which it was painted, the subject was rather a cruel one, representing as it did the putting to rout of a large body of mounted Frenchmen by a handful of English cavalry; but it greatly tickled King Henry's fancy, and he made a point of drawing the attention of the Ambassadors to it. This picture has disappeared.

RETURN TO BASLE

Holbein was back in Basle in the summer of 1528. Possibly he was recalled by the Town Council, under penalty of losing his rights of citizenship if he disobeyed. On August 29 he purchased for 300 florins a house overlooking the Rhine, and on March 30, 1531, he also bought the adjoining house for 70 florins, thus proving that his English visit had been far from fruitless. He remained in Basle for four years, but the only important work upon which he was engaged was the completion of his Town Hall decorations. The Town Council requested him to finish the "back wall," and he covered it with two fine compositions, *The Meeting of Samuel and Saul*, and *Rehoboam*, the preliminary sketches for which are now in the Basle Museum. He was engaged upon this work during the latter half of 1530.

Basle was still torn by religious dissensions, but the party of the Reformation now held the upper hand. A furious outbreak in 1529 led to the further destruction of religious paintings and sculpture. Even Holbein did not escape at least minor persecution for his religious principles. On June 18, 1530, he was, in conjunction with a number of his fellow-citizens, called upon to explain why he had not taken part in the communion service instituted by the Basle Church after the abolition of the Catholic creed in the previous year. He cautiously replied that before approaching the Lord's Table he desired the signification of the holy mystery to be more clearly explained to him; and this seems to have been done, as he did not persist in his refusal. Beyond the Town Hall decorations he does not seem to have found much profitable work to do. He painted a portrait of his wife and two children (Basle Museum) and a new portrait of *Erasmus* in 1530, the small round one now at Basle, the original source of a number of copies at Parma, Turin, and elsewhere. There was little opportunity, however, for him to follow his art with adequate success, and his thoughts naturally turned once more towards England. He came back to this country in 1532, probably without informing the Basle authorities of his intention. They sent a very flattering letter after him, offering him a fixed salary if he would return, but he does not appear to have taken any immediate notice of this suggestion.

SECOND RESIDENCE IN ENGLAND

During Holbein's absence Sir Thomas More had become Lord Chancellor, but this office he relinquished in May, 1532, and was gradually falling out of favour with the King. Holbein did not take up his residence in Chelsea again, but settled in London, near the large colony of German and Netherlandish merchants then forming an important part of the commercial life of the capital. These merchants of the Hanseatic League formed a close corporation among themselves, and in their midst Holbein now made his home. Their place of meeting was called the Steelyard, and here their warehouses and residences were grouped round the hall of the guild, with its trim garden and special wineshop. Among them the artist found not only the language and habits of his own country, but also plenty of well-paid employment.

During 1532 and 1533, and occasionally later, he painted a number of his compatriots seated in their offices and engaged in the ordinary routine of business life, including the superb picture of *Georg Gisze* (Berlin, *see illustration*), *Hans of Antwerp*, the goldsmith, later on one of Holbein's executors (Windsor), *Derich Born* (Windsor and Munich), *Derich Berck* (Petworth), *Geryck Tybis* (Vienna), *Ambrose Fallen* (Brunswick), and several others whose names have not been discovered. He was also employed by the members of the Steelyard as a corporate body. At the coronation of Anne Boleyn, in May, 1533, the streets of London were gaily decorated by the various city companies and guilds, and the triumphal arch erected by the Hanseatic League was designed by Holbein. Still more important were the two large allegorical paintings in monochrome, *The Triumph of Riches* and *The Triumph of Poverty*, with which he decorated their banqueting-hall. These fine works have disappeared. Fortunately, they were copied by Zucchero in 1574, and by Jan de Bisschop (British Museum), while the original sketch for *The Triumph of Riches* is in the Louvre.

Holbein had now reached the highest point of his career, and the series of brilliant portraits he produced during the last ten years of his life is unrivalled. It was probably owing to his connection with the Steelyard that he was employed by several foreign Ambassadors, who were accredited to England during his second residence here. Many of these German merchants were more than mere traders. Owing to their knowledge of foreign languages, and their business relations with all parts of the world, they were often employed by the Government, and occasionally sent on important missions abroad. In this way they were personally known to many of the Ambassadors to England.

In 1533 Holbein produced his most important work still in this country, the picture familiarly known as *The Ambassadors* (*see illustration*), representing Jean de Dinteville, French Ambassador at the English Court, and his friend George de Selve, Bishop of Lavaur. Another magnificent portrait of an Ambassador was painted about this time, probably in 1534, the famous one in the Dresden Gallery, for many years said to be a masterpiece of Leonardo da Vinci, and a portrait of Ludovico Sforza, and still called in the Dresden catalogue *Hubert Morett, Goldsmith to Henry VIII*. It really represents *Charles de Solier, Comte de Morette*, who was in England more than once, and succeeded Dinteville as resident Ambassador in 1534. His clients, however, were not only foreigners; he constantly painted Englishmen of all ranks and classes. In 1533 he produced the fine portrait of *Robert Cheseman, of Dormanswell* (Hague), with his hawk on his wrist, erroneously called *The King's Falconer* (*see illustration*), and the equally fine one of a man in black (Berlin), supposed to be a member of the Trelawney family. The latter's brother he had painted in the previous year (Count Schönborn's Collection, Vienna). In 1534 we have the portrait of that "hammer of the monks," Thomas Cromwell, when only Master of the Jewel House.

It is not until 1536 that we get any actual proof that Holbein was in the King's service. In that year he painted the new Queen, Jane Seymour (Vienna and Woburn Abbey). It seems certain, however, that Henry must have been well aware of his artistic capacity before this date. A number of artists, both foreign and native, all greatly inferior to Holbein, were then employed by the King, and professional jealousy may have had some share in retarding his entry into the royal service. During Holbein's first visit to England John Browne was sergeant-painter to the King, holding the office for more than twenty years. He was succeeded by another Englishman, Andrew Wright, who in his turn was followed by an Italian, Antonio Toto; but, next to Holbein, the leading painter in England, and a man of real ability, was Lucas Horembault, or Hornebolt, of Ghent, who had settled here with his father Gerard and his sister Susannah, both of them artists. The salary that Hornebolt received from the King was always larger than that paid to Holbein.

In 1537 Holbein painted a great picture on the wall of the Privy Chamber at Whitehall, representing the two Kings, Henry VII. and Henry VIII., and their Queens, Elizabeth of York and Jane Seymour. When the art historian,

Van Mander, saw it in 1604, it was still in perfect preservation, and he speaks with the utmost enthusiasm about it. It was destroyed in the fire which burned down that palace in 1698. Happily, there still exists a small copy of it (Hampton Court), which was made in 1667 by Remigius van Leemput by order of Charles II., and Mr. Ernest Law has recently discovered a replica by the same painter; while a still better judgment can be formed of its size, composition, and general effect from Holbein's cartoon for the left half, showing the King and his father, which belongs to the Duke of Devonshire. It is a black chalk drawing, heightened with Indian ink, and was used for tracing the design upon the wall.

Almost every other portrait of Henry painted after 1537—and there are many of them scattered about England and on the Continent—was based upon the Whitehall likeness. It is very doubtful if even one of them is the genuine work of Holbein's brush. Such portraits were multiplied to give away to foreign Princes and faithful subjects. The best of them is the well-known full-face representation of the King in Warwick Castle—a life-size work, very admirably painted, most probably by Hornebolt. There is really no authentic portrait of him by Holbein in existence, with the exception of the rough chalk drawing at Munich and the exquisite square portrait at Althorp, which, in the opinion of Mr. Lionel Cust, F.S.A., is a genuine example.

After the death of Jane Seymour, the Privy Council lost no moment in urging the King to marry again. The choice fell upon Christina, daughter of the King of Denmark, and niece of the Emperor Charles V. She was Duchess of Milan, and the young widow of Francesco Sforza, the last Duke of his race. Holbein went over to Brussels in March, 1538, to paint the lady's portrait. The very lovely full-length portrait of this Princess belongs to the Duke of Norfolk, who has generously lent it to the National Gallery for a number of years (*see illustration*). This is, perhaps, the most perfect piece of portraiture Holbein ever accomplished, and one of the great pictures of the world.

At this time the artist was receiving a salary of £30 a year from the King in the form of a retaining fee, and he must have obtained further payment for whatever work he did. His money was paid quarterly, but he was occasionally granted a whole year's salary in advance. In the autumn of the same year, 1538, he made a second journey abroad, to Upper Burgundy, for which he received £10 from the King's purse, probably to obtain a second sitting from the Duchess. He took this opportunity of paying a flying visit to Basle, no doubt to talk over with the Town Council an offer they had just made him of a pension of fifty gulden, with leave of absence in England for two years longer, if he would then return to his native city and settle there. He remained in Basle for only a few days during December, and was received with enthusiasm by his fellow-citizens. He most probably returned to England by way of Paris, where he stopped to apprentice his eldest son Philip to the goldsmith Jerome David. Whatever agreement he may have made with the Swiss authorities, he did not visit Basle again during the five remaining years of his life. He was back in London on New Year's Day, 1539, and presented a portrait of the young Prince Edward to the King.

In August, 1539, he was again sent abroad upon a similar mission. He went to Düren, in the Duchy of Cleves, to paint the daughters of the Duke, a Protestant Prince, with whom, since the negotiations with the Emperor for Christina's hand had come to nothing, Cromwell thought an alliance would be politic. The likeness Holbein made of *Anne of Cleves*, probably the fine one now in the Louvre, is said by tradition to have so flattered the lady that Henry consented to marry her, with the well-known disastrous results.

With the exception of a miniature at Windsor, there is no authentic portrait of *Catherine Howard*, whom the King married as soon as he had divorced the unfortunate Anne; but her uncle, *Thomas Howard, third Duke of Norfolk*, the Lord High Admiral, was painted by him more than once. Holbein had now become the most popular portrait painter of the day, and his commissions were very numerous. It is impossible to give a complete list of them here, but the principal ones will be found in the Appendix.

At Windsor Castle is the magnificent collection of chalk drawings of heads, over eighty in number, which includes portraits of many of the most illustrious people of the day. These were preliminary studies for portraits, and are the finest record we possess of the celebrities of the Tudor period, invaluable both historically and artistically. In them Holbein is seen at his finest as a delineator of character.

In 1542 he began the large painting which was ordered to commemorate the granting of a charter by Henry VIII. to the newly-incorporated Company of Barber Surgeons, which still hangs in the Company's Hall in London. He did not live to complete it. Some of the heads of the principal physicians he had finished, but the greater part of the picture, including the huge and ugly figure of the King, out of all proportion to the other persons represented, was put in by some other and far inferior hand. At least two of the doctors represented in this work were also painted by him separately, *Dr. John Chambers* (Vienna) and *Sir William Butts*, as well as the latter's wife.

Holbein died in the following year, 1543, carried off by the plague, which then raged in London. The exact date of his death is not known, but he made a hasty will on October 7, and on November 29 administration was granted to his old friend Hans of Antwerp, the goldsmith. He was living at the time in the parish of St. Andrew Undershaft, where he was rated as a foreigner. He is supposed to have been buried in the Church of St. Katherine Cree, but no record of this has been discovered. His wife died in 1549. His eldest son Philip, "a good, well-behaved lad," served his apprenticeship in Paris, and finally settled in Augsburg, founding that branch of the family upon which the Emperor Matthias conferred a patent of nobility as the Holbeins of Holbeinsberg. His second son James died as a goldsmith in London, while his daughters married respectable citizens of Basle.

THE ART OF HOLBEIN

HOLBEIN'S art was many-sided, although, during the latter half of his life, he was occupied chiefly with portraiture. This was not owing to the artist's preference for this mode of expression, but to the fact that there was very little demand for any other form of painting in England. The painter of *The Meyer Madonna* was not the man to have abandoned the production of large religious compositions if there had been any adequate demand for them. His few works of this nature which remain place him in the front rank of sixteenth-century artists, and, if he had been born on the south side of the Alps, he would have painted sacred pictures as fine as those of any Italian cinquecentist; even Raphael would have found in him a worthy rival.

It is an immense loss to art that all his large decorative undertakings, and many of his most important pictures, have perished or have been lost, so that to-day we can only judge of them by a few preliminary studies, certain fragments of the originals which have been preserved in museums, and, in a few cases, some early and careful copies of a reduced size. The decorations with which he covered a number of houses in Lucerne and Basle have all disappeared. What the weather did not ruin the clumsy hand of the restorer and street-improver has destroyed. A number of his sacred pictures must have perished during the artist's lifetime through the fury of iconoclastic mobs. Damp, dirt, and neglect were the cause of the gradual fading away of his wall-paintings in the interior of the Basle Town Hall. His two great allegorical works for the decoration of the dining-hall of the Steelyard—*The Triumph of Riches* and *The Triumph of Poverty*—have vanished, either destroyed in the Whitehall fire of 1698 or dispersed at the sale of Charles I.'s pictures. Some such fate seems also to have befallen the great portrait group of *Sir Thomas More's Family*. The great wall-painting in the Privy Chamber in Whitehall was also destroyed by fire. Gone, too, is *The Battle of Spurs*, which, if Mr. Nicholls is right, was painted by our artist. Finally, death cut short the painting of the picture in the Barber Surgeons' Hall. Such a list of lost or ruined masterpieces is, unhappily, not uncommon in the history of art, but Holbein has suffered more than most men; yet enough remains from his brush to allow us to place him among the greatest men of genius of his own or any succeeding age.

As already stated, he owed little to any other master than his father. It is impossible to say to what extent he assisted the elder painter in the series of sacred pictures now preserved in Augsburg and elsewhere in Germany, although certain critics hold that he took a large share in the production of *The Martyrdom of St. Sebastian* in Munich. This picture is the elder Holbein's masterpiece, and in it, more than in any other of his works, he has thrown off the German mediævalism in which he was trained, and has emulated the newer style of the Renaissance, with its fine flowing lines and rounded forms and its exact imitation of Nature. It was to this German painter of repute that Holbein was indebted for almost all the artistic training he received. His painting was not affected to any extent by other artists except, indirectly, by the Italians of the North; but what was talent in the father became genius of the rarest quality in the son.

LARGE DECORATIVE WORKS AND WALL-PAINTINGS

The practice of decorating both the exterior and the interior of houses with large wall-paintings, so universal throughout Italy in the sixteenth century, was by no means uncommon north of the Alps; but in Germany this class of work was badly paid, and the painter employed made use of much mechanical assistance, and did not lavish too much personal care upon it. No other Northern artist carried out work of this nature with such brilliancy and such success as Holbein. It is probable that the subjects of his wall-paintings were chosen for him by his patrons to suit their own tastes; but his fertility of imagination was so great that his renderings of the selected themes were stamped with his original genius. The designs were not carried out by him in a slipshod manner, without understanding, but were masterpieces of dramatic power and composition, and, no doubt, equally artistic in their colour schemes.

In his decorations for the house of Jacob von Hertenstein, in Lucerne, many of the subjects were taken from ancient times. The façade was covered with scenes from secular history, pageants, and combats of children, in a setting of florid Renaissance architecture, an important feature being a great triumphal procession of Cæsar, in its main lines copied from Mantegna. In the interior the walls of the chapel were covered with religious paintings, and the largest chamber was given up to hunting scenes with landscape backgrounds and a representation of *The Fountain of Youth*, with many humorous details.

There is no doubt that he decorated a number of houses in Basle in a similar manner, though we have records of only one of them; but drawings of several elaborately ornamented façades are preserved in various collections, which show that he was often occupied with this kind of work in his younger days. The most famous of these decorated buildings was, as already stated, known as *The House of the Dance*, from a broad frieze running across the second story, which represented a number of peasants boisterously dancing to the music of the bagpipes. The whole front was embellished with painted Renaissance architecture. The great variety of subjects he included, and the elaborate details, may be studied in a sketch preserved in the Basle Museum.

The subjects chosen for the interior decoration of the Basle Town Hall were also from classical antiquity. Richly ornamented columns divided the walls into a number of spaces, which were filled with paintings representing the vital importance to a community of impartial justice. Holbein's subjects were *Charondas, the Lawgiver, plunging the Sword into his own Heart; Zaleucus ordering his own Right Eye to be torn out instead of his Son's; Curius Dentatus sending back the Ambassadors of the Samnites;* and *Sapor, King of Persia, using the Body of the captured Emperor Valerian as a step from which to mount his Horse.* The smaller panels were single figures, such as *Christ, David, Justice, Wisdom,* and *Moderation.* The remaining wall in the Hall, painted in 1530, was covered with two large Biblical subjects—*Rehoboam dismissing the Messengers of the Israelites with fierce threats,* and *The meeting of Samuel and Saul,* when the Prophet angrily reproves the King for having disobeyed the command of God in sparing the Amalekites. The original sketches for both these compositions still exist, and are sufficient to prove how fine the completed pictures must have been. The vehement gesture of Rehoboam is well conceived, and the composition of the Samuel and Saul is masterly.

The two large allegorical friezes for the banquet-room of the Steelyard merchants in London must have been equally fine. The original sketch for *The Triumph of Riches* (Louvre) shows how easily the genius of the artist adapted itself to this kind of work. The figures in these two compositions, which were done in *tempera* on canvas, were life-size. They soon became famous, and in 1574 were copied by Zucchero, who, according to Carl van Mander, declared they were as fine as anything accomplished by Raphael. Such triumphal processions as these were, of course, a favourite method of decoration in his day, of which Mantegna's *Triumph of Cæsar* was the most famous. In *The Triumph of Riches* he depicted Plutus, God of Wealth, seated in a car drawn by four horses, with Fortune in front, her veil flying behind her, scattering gold among the accompanying crowd, which is made up of many men of antiquity famous for their wealth, luxury, or avarice. In *The Triumph of Poverty* Poverty herself, an ancient and miserable hag, and her comrade, Misfortune, are drawn in a poor barrow by two asses, Stupidity and Inactivity, and two oxen, Negligence and Sloth. The vehicle is driven by Hope, who is accompanied by Industry, Memory, and Experience, who distribute axe or hammer, spade or flail, symbols of work, among the poverty-stricken people who crowd round.

In all these large decorative works Holbein displayed the greatest fertility of invention, and a power of composition of a very high order. The sense of life and movement in all the figures, and the appropriateness of the gestures, are alike admirable. In some of his wall-paintings he showed a keen sense of humour; and that joy of life, as felt by the Teuton of his day in his moments of relaxation and merriment, is admirably expressed. There is, too, an exuberance of invention in the architectural and ornamental details which is one of the most striking features of this side of his art, showing how quickly and completely he had made the new ideas of the Renaissance his own.

RELIGIOUS PAINTINGS

Holbein's religious pictures almost all date from the earlier part of his career, and few remain which are works of his maturity. More than one of them perished, there is little doubt, during the stormy days of the Reformation in Basle. His earliest known picture is a small panel of *The Virgin and Child*, dated 1514, a work of great promise for a youth of seventeen. It displays a real, though naïve, charm, and the tender attitude with which the Virgin holds the Child is very attractive. She is dressed in white, with a black cloak, and her long, fair hair falls over her shoulders, and Holbein seems to have taken an especial delight in the careful painting of it. This little work, tentative as it is in many ways, gives signs that the hand which painted it was soon to become that of a master. Other early works of a similar character are *The Virgin Mary* and *St. John the Evangelist*, quarter lengths, seen against a blue background, which remained the artist's favourite setting for his heads throughout his life. The series of five pictures on canvas, taken from *The Passion of Christ*, need not detain us. It is probable that they were hastily painted for some church decoration or religious celebration. Among the numerous designs for glass-painting which he made in Basle, the most important is a series of ten designs illustrating *The Passion of Christ*, each one set in a background of elaborate architectural structure. The scenes are simply treated, but with great dramatic power, if not with great depth of feeling. The action in most of them is finely conceived, and many of the figures have both dignity and beauty.

Holbein took the same subject, *The Passion of Christ*, for an altar-piece consisting of eight small panels (Basle Museum). For more than 200 years this work was considered to be the artist's finest achievement, and it was preserved in the Basle Town Hall until 1777, when the Town Council presented it to the Museum, and had it thoroughly restored before handing it over, with most disastrous results. The abominably gaudy colours which were then daubed upon it have taken away most of the charm which graced it when it first left the master's hands. It is still possible, however, to form some judgment of its composition, and to see how skilfully the artist has managed the light and shade. The eight scenes are combined in one frame in a very effective and harmonious manner, forming one picturesque whole. Each little picture, taken by itself, is a work of art and of real beauty. Two other panels in the Minster of Freiburg, somewhat similar to the above in the exceptionally successful and picturesque arrangement of the lighting, form the wings of an altar-piece, of which the centre panel has disappeared. They were painted for Hans Oberreidt, one of the Basle Town Councillors, and represent *The Nativity* and *The Adoration of the Magi*, with the donor and the numerous members of his family kneeling below. All the figures are small, while the backgrounds are large and imposing. Another little work of great beauty, and important as being the only sacred painting by Holbein now in England, is the *Noli Me Tangere* at Hampton Court.

A very remarkable picture of *The Dead Christ* (Basle) was painted in 1521. The nude body lies in a narrow tomb of marble, open at the side. Except for the stigmata, there is very little religious signification in it. The painful subject has been in no way idealized; it is, on the contrary, one of the most vividly realistic paintings of a dead man ever produced by a great painter.

The picture known as *The Solothurn Madonna*, painted in the following year, is one of Holbein's two finest religious paintings. It is now in the possession of Herr Zetter, but was, no doubt, originally a commission for the Minster of Solothurn. It represents the Virgin and Child between St. Martin of Tours and St. Ursus. The Virgin is seated with the Child on her knee under an open arch, and her figure stands out against the blue sky which is seen through it. Her face is very sweet and sympathetic. The naked Child, with its little arms stretched out, is a delightful piece of portraiture, while the two saints are magnificent figures. This picture, deeply reverent in feeling, is conceived with great simplicity, but is very noble in sentiment.

The Meyer Madonna, in Darmstadt, Holbein's greatest masterpiece of religious painting, and one of the finest sacred pictures in the world.

BOOK ILLUSTRATIONS AND ORNAMENTAL WOODCUTS

Holbein's versatility as an artist is nowhere shown more convincingly than in the illustrations he made for printed books, and the series of woodcuts which were published from his designs during the last decade of his life. His title-pages, initial letters, chapter headings, and ornamental borders, for Froben and other printers, display a rich invention, greatly in advance of most similar work of that period. In some of them the artist's sureness of hand and firmness of drawing have been sadly blunted by the incapacity of the woodcutter. In others, however, he was very happily associated with a cutter of real genius, Hans Lützelburger, who had both the skill and intuition to carry out the master's intentions with marvellous and sympathetic accuracy. One of the most celebrated of his title-pages is that known as *The Table of Cebes*, representing, by means of countless little figures, the soul's journey through life.

But Holbein's fame as a designer of woodcuts, which had spread throughout Europe before the end of the sixteenth century, was based

[*Darmstadt* Hanfstängl photo.] THE MEYER MADONNA.

upon two celebrated series of designs, *The Dance of Death* and his *Old Testament Illustrations*, in which his gifts as an illustrator are most clearly shown. *The Dance of Death*, with its forty little pictures, at once became popular, and editions followed one after the other, with additional illustrations. The subject was a very favourite one throughout mediæval Europe, and in Holbein it reaches its highest development. It is a series of short pictorial sermons, in which the artist points out to the reader how slight and how uncertain is his hold upon life, and how in the presence of death both Prince and peasant are equal. In the satire with which Holbein has treated clerics of all degrees we learn something of the way in which the Reformation influenced him. Each little picture is a masterpiece of art, in which is depicted, with grim humour, death's unexpected approach, sparing neither King nor Pontiff, Queen nor courtesan, knight nor beggar, old age nor childhood. In each one the feeling for fine dramatic situation is admirable, the whole being indicated in a few sure lines of masterly draughtsmanship. Detailed accounts of each of the subjects will be found in Dr. Woltmann's "Holbein and His Time," and in Chatto and Jackson's "History of Wood Engraving," while Ruskin's "Ariadne Florentina" should be read for a very sympathetic and beautiful analysis of their intellectual side, their spiritual meaning, and Holbein's marvellous power of design for such work.

In the same year, 1538, his illustrations to the Old Testament, ninety-one in all, were also published by the brothers Trechsel. They did not accompany an edition of the Bible, but were issued as a book of pictures, with appropriate letter-press. They are less known than *The Dance of Death* woodcuts, and in them the artist has put a curb on his fertile imagination, and confines himself to telling the sacred stories with great simplicity and directness, while nothing essential to the full understanding of the story is omitted.

In addition to these more important woodcuts, Holbein also designed several series of ornamental alphabets, one of them a dance of death, another with peasants at their merrymakings, and a third with children at their games.

DESIGNS FOR GOLDSMITHS
AND OTHER CRAFTSMEN

No form of art came amiss to this versatile genius. He made hundreds of designs for jewellers and metal-workers, many of which, happily, have been preserved, the greater part of them being now in the Basle and British Museums. These include designs for rings, brooches, pendants, medallions, buttons, badges, jewelled monograms, hand-mirrors, decorative bands to be engraved upon metal, dagger handles and sheaths, and every kind of personal ornament, and a number of larger objects, such as cups, bowls, clocks, and similar pieces. In these, again, his most inventive powers of design, based upon Renaissance lines, combined with a very skilful adaptation for decorative purposes of the human figure, place him in the forefront of sixteenth-century designers. His most important piece of goldsmith's work of which we know was a gold cup of beautiful Renaissance design, known as the *Jane Seymour Cup*, the original drawing for which is in the British Museum, and a second one in the University Galleries at Oxford. It was undoubtedly made as a gift from the King to the Queen, and bears their initials, together with Jane Seymour's motto, "Bound to obey and serve." Benvenuto Cellini never accomplished anything finer in cinquecento ornament than this. In the beauty of his design, with its more restrained taste, Holbein equalled the famous Italian craftsman. Another beautiful design for a clock, in which the nude figures of boys are admirably introduced, was completed for Sir Anthony Denny, who presented it to the King on the New Year's Day immediately following the artist's death.

In his younger days, when in Basle, he made many admirable designs for stained and painted glass windows, some with sacred subjects, already mentioned, others with armorial bearings, and in several the figures of armed soldiers, with their picturesque costumes, are introduced with excellent effect.

Among the many drawings by him which have been preserved there are several examples of architecture, of which the most important is a drawing of a large fireplace and chimney-piece, decorated with the Royal Arms and of very elaborate Renaissance design (British Museum), but whether it was actually carried out is uncertain. Several architectural works have been attributed to him, such as the old Whitehall Gateway, now demolished, the so-called "Holbein Porch" and lodge at Wilton, the carved capitals in the More Chapel at Chelsea, and a ceiling in Whitehall, mentioned very vaguely by Samuel Pepys. It is almost certain that he had nothing whatever to do with these, although his fertility in the invention of architectural details for the backgrounds of his pictures and woodcuts was so great that possibly he wanted only an opportunity to attempt more serious architectural work, as was the custom of many Italian artists, who built as well as painted.

PORTRAIT PAINTING

It was, however, as a portrait painter that Holbein's genius reached its highest manifestations. In portraiture he stands side by side with the greatest. That so considerable a part of his time was given up to this branch of art was no doubt owing to environment, although his stupendous gifts in this direction were born in him, and were bound to come to the front. The Reformation in Switzerland brought his paintings of altar-pieces to an abrupt conclusion, and in England he found no demand for sacred art, but, on the other hand, a splendid field for portrait painting, of which he availed himself to the utmost; and he has left a series of lifelike representations of the illustrious men and women of Henry VIII.'s reign of more value, both historically and as absolutely faithful representations of the people depicted, than even the similar series painted by Van Dyck at the Court of Charles I., or by Reynolds and Gainsborough under George II. and George III., and even wider in its range of subjects than Velasquez accomplished in Philip's service. The magical brush of the artist has pictured for us, with a living realism, many members of the royal House of Tudor, high prelates of the Church, leading statesmen, soldiers and sailors, men of learning and of science, leaders of fashion, country gentlemen and their wives, German and English merchants, foreign diplomatists, and plain citizens.

One of the greatest artistic treasures in this country is the series of drawings of heads at Windsor Castle, the preliminary studies Holbein made before painting his portraits, and, slight as many of them are, themselves most vivid portraits, in which, with wonderful swiftness yet sureness of touch, he has given us not only an accurate likeness, but also the character which lies behind the face-mask, allowing us to look into the inmost thoughts of each sitter, and so to fathom the invisible by the aid of his acute penetration, which is of far higher value than mere accurate delineation of features, and is the crowning quality of all really great portraiture.

In all his completed portraits he spared no pains over the painting of accessories and details, and in some of them he carried this to as fine a finish as any Dutchman or Fleming ever accomplished. What could be finer than the various objects scattered about the office of the Steelyard merchant, *Georg Gisze* (Berlin), or the ornaments and embroideries, silks, satins, and furs of the dresses in such portraits as those of *Archbishop Wareham* (Louvre), *Jane Seymour* (Vienna), *Anne of Cleves* (Louvre), *Charles de Solier, Comte de Morette* (Dresden), *The Ambassadors* (National Gallery), or the *Duke of Norfolk* (Windsor)? Yet the fine execution of all this elaborate detail is soon overlooked, and attention is fixed solely upon the portrait itself, in which, without any apparent effort on the part of the artist, the very man stands out before us exactly as he looked when in the flesh, with no flattering or softening of harsh features, and with his character, and the thoughts which he imagined were hidden from the painter, laid bare for our inspection.

Holbein produces this effect of truth and this revelation of character by what appear to be the simplest methods, which yet are in reality most subtle and most profound. He puts but little of himself into his portraits, and almost everything of his sitter. No great subtleties of light and shade are brought in to aid the artistic result; and even colour, delightful and harmonious in a high degree as Holbein's colour always is, is not allowed to usurp the attention from the purpose of the work, the complete realization of both the outward and inner man. What at the first glance seems almost an unnatural flatness in his painting of a face displays upon examination the most delicate and accurate modelling of form. His keenness of observation was extraordinary. He constantly noted the slight difference in the shape of two sides of a face, and that a man's eyes were not always of the same size, characteristics which even the best artists have sometimes failed to see. His painting of hair and of beards displays a marvellous fidelity to nature, and his drawing of hands, and the expression he puts into them, is extraordinary. In the painting of eyes, too, and mouth he is most expressive. The hands of *Erasmus* in the Louvre and at Longford Castle, of *Wareham* and *Anne of Cleves* in the Louvre, are instances of this; and the eyes of *Southwell* (Uffizi), and of *Cheseman* (Hague), and both eyes, hands, and mouth of the *Duchess of Milan* (National Gallery).

He is seen at his best as a portrait painter in the *Duchess of Milan* (*see illustration*); *Count Morette*; Jacob Meyer and his family in the Madonna picture at Darmstadt (*see illustration*); *Erasmus* at Longford Castle (*see illustration*) and in the Louvre; *Georg Gisze* (*see illustration*); the portrait of an unknown man with a long beard, formerly belonging to Sir J. E. Millais, at Berlin; the portraits of three unknown young men, all dated 1541, at Vienna, the Hague, and Berlin; *The Ambassadors*; *The Two Godsalves* at Dresden; his own wife and children at Basle; and the *Anne of Cleves, Robert Cheseman* (*see illustration*), and *Richard Southwell* already mentioned; while among his earliest portraits those of *Bonifacius Amerbach*, and *Jacob Meyer and His Wife* on one panel, both in Basle, should be carefully studied. A number of others might be mentioned, but these are sufficient to establish his right to the title of a great master.

Holbein's method of work seems to have remained the same throughout his life. It was his custom to make a preliminary study of the head on paper, fixing with unerring accuracy the features of the sitter, and making notes as to the colour or the details of the ornaments to be introduced at the side of the drawing, and for the rest relying almost entirely upon his memory, which must have been singularly retentive. In this way he could accomplish much without fatiguing his patrons with a number of sittings. Occasionally, by the use of colour and more careful and elaborate drawing, he carried such preliminary studies much further, until they were finished portraits in themselves. Others, again, are only hasty outlines, but displaying the hand of a master. They were executed in charcoal and black and red chalk, the eyes, hair, and hand being often drawn in their proper colours. Some are strengthened in the outlines with the brush and Indian ink, while in others the whole face has been modelled with the brush with the greatest delicacy. In some cases he fixed the preliminary drawing upon a panel, and then painted the finished portrait over it.

Unlike that of Dürer, the one other really great German painter, Holbein's art bears no traces of mediævalism, either in form, in method, or in thought. He was in every way a child of the Renaissance, and so was essentially modern, as we understand the term to-day. For this reason the forms in which he expresses himself require no explanation or preliminary training for their full comprehension, but are immediately intelligible to us. The great Franconian, Albert Dürer, was steeped in the spirit of mediævalism, a dreamer of dreams, full of philosophical theories and spiritual speculation, and his work fired with a passion which Holbein's lacked; whereas the great Swabian was before all things a serene painter, lacking strong artistic passions. He loved Nature simply and for herself, and had the keenest vision for her manifold beauties down to the minutest details, and was filled with the delight of life and joy of the world around him, without troubling himself greatly about theological questions. That he was at heart on the side of the Reformation is shown in many of his woodcut illustrations, but his share in the controversy is marked by none of the violence which characterized the eager partisans on either side.

Sir Frederic Leighton, speaking of these two painters in his address to the Royal Academy students in 1893, notes the most striking differences between them in a few admirable sentences. He says of Holbein: "As a draughtsman he displayed a flow, a fulness of form, and an almost classic restraint which are wanting in the work of Dürer, and are, indeed, not found elsewhere in German art. As a colourist he had a keen sense of the values of tone relations, a sense in which Dürer again was lacking; not so Teutonic in every way as the Nuremberg master, he formed a link between the Italian and German races. A less powerful personality than Dürer, he was a far superior painter. Proud may that country be indeed that counts two names so great in art."

It is an almost impossible task to sum up in a short paragraph the leading characteristics of Holbein's art. In his great decorative wall-paintings he rivalled many of the best Italian painters of the Renaissance. In the depth of expression in his portraits, and his power of rendering character and grasping the hidden thoughts of his sitter, he is worthy of a place by Leonardo da Vinci. In his religious paintings he reached at least once, in *The Meyer Madonna*, the level upon which Raphael stood, and had his surroundings been different he would have attained signal success as a painter of sacred compositions. He attempted no great subtleties of chiaroscuro, nor sought to rival his Italian contemporaries in the magnificence of their colour; but his colour is always most harmonious, and both in design and style he was great.

In his most important designs for metal-workers he is equal to Benvenuto, that most inspired and artistic of swashbucklers, and with more restraint in the handling of his theme, but no less invention. With the exception of Dürer, no artist of the cinquecento produced such admirable designs for woodcuts and book illustrations. In his preliminary drawings for his portraits the insight, the ease of draughtsmanship, the force united with the greatest delicacy, and the freedom from all traces of mannerism, unite to make them—as seen at Windsor, Basle, Berlin, and elsewhere— one of the most complete and valuable series of documents of the history of the first half of the sixteenth century we possess to-day. Possibly the greatest side of his genius is to be found in his penetrative power into the very souls of his sitters, and the revelation of true character which was the consequence of it. This keen insight, aided by a manipulative skill of a very rare quality, combined to make him one of the great masters of the world. Ruskin's judgment of him, when comparing him with Sir Joshua Reynolds, may be fitly quoted in conclusion. He says: "The work of Holbein is true and thorough, accomplished in the highest, as the most literal, sense, with a calm entireness of unaffected resolution which sacrifices nothing, forgets nothing, and fears nothing. Holbein is complete; what he sees, he sees with his whole soul; what he paints, he paints with his whole might."

OUR ILLUSTRATIONS

AMONG the many splendid portraits which Holbein painted it is difficult to make a selection for the purpose of illustration. *The Meyer Madonna* has been included as his finest religious painting and his most celebrated work. Although the *Portrait of the Duchess of Milan* and *The Ambassadors* are now in the National Gallery, and so are accessible to all, they have been reproduced, because the first is in many ways the best portrait, and certainly the most fascinating Holbein ever accomplished, while the second is the most important work of the master now remaining in England. The other portraits reproduced in this book are all in their way masterpieces of portraiture, and the *Noli Me Tangere*, at Hampton Court, is of interest as the only sacred picture by him which is now in this country.

The Meyer Madonna in the old schloss of Darmstadt, belonging to the Grand Duke of Hesse, is one of the great sacred pictures of the world. It represents the Burgomaster of Basle, Jacob Meyer, and his family kneeling in adoration at the feet of the Virgin Mary, who stands in an architectural niche of red marble and gray stone, with a shell-shaped canopy over her head. Her dress is blue, but the darkening of the varnish has given it a greenish hue, with a bright red girdle and a large mantle, which is spread out protectingly over the donors. She is placed upon no isolated throne, but stands among the Meyer family, as though to protect them from evil. The Divine Child in her arms leans back with His head against her breast, while His left hand is stretched out over the suppliants as though in benediction. On one side Meyer kneels, his hands clasped in prayer, gazing fervently upwards, while his young son is occupied in supporting a little naked child who stands in the front. On the other side kneel the women-folk, with the daughter, Anna, nearest the spectator, her golden head-dress elaborately embroidered with pearls. Next to her is her mother, Meyer's second wife, Dorothea Kannegiesser, and nearest the Virgin a third woman, who may be either his first wife, Magdalen Bär, or Magdalen's daughter by a previous marriage. All are kneeling on a richly coloured Turkish carpet. The figures are about three-quarters the size of life. The colour of the whole is rich, subdued, and very fine.

The Dresden Gallery possesses a very fine copy of this picture, with certain alterations, which, until the two pictures were exhibited side by side in 1871, was considered by most critics to be the original work. It is now acknowledged to be only a skilful copy, probably done about one hundred years later, when Meyer's descendants sold the picture to an Amsterdam dealer about 1626. Certain alterations have been made by the copyist in the hope of improving the picture. In the original the head of the Virgin comes too near to the top of the niche, and this has been remedied, and he has tried to improve and beautify Mary's somewhat thick-set figure, resulting in a lack of natural force and a weak idealization which Holbein himself would have scorned. The happy-looking Child of the Darmstadt picture has been copied so badly and with so unhappy an expression that it has been thought to represent a sick child, and it is probably owing to this that a number of fanciful interpretations have been given of the hidden meaning of the picture. Both in colour and in effect the copy in no way equals the original, which is in all ways a picture of noble simplicity, splendid colour, and striking veracity of portraiture. The Darmstadt picture was painted about 1526. Meyer was a banker and money-changer, and during the struggles of the Reformation remained a staunch Catholic, and no doubt ordered this altar-piece as an outward sign of the faith that was in him.

For reasons already mentioned a number of suggestions, more or less improbable, have been made as to the inner meaning of the painting. It has been suggested that it is a votive picture to commemorate the recovery of a sick child. This idea is carried still further by others, who say that the infant in the Madonna's arms is the soul of a dead child, while a third interpretation is that it

[*National Gallery.* Hanfstängl photo.] THE AMBASSADORS.

is the soul of the woman kneeling next to the Virgin, who is supposed to have recently died. Other explanations have been given, but they are all sentimental refinements of modern German criticism, first voiced by Tieck and Schlegel, which might not have occurred to them if they had studied the original instead of the copy. Ruskin was on the side of the sentimentalists. He says (*Cornhill Magazine*, 1860): "The received tradition respecting the Holbein Madonna is beautiful, and I believe the interpretation to be true. A father and mother have prayed to her for the life of their sick child. She appears to them, her own Child in her arms. She puts down her Christ before them, takes their child into her arms instead; it lies down upon her bosom, and stretches its hands to its father and mother, saying farewell." The simplest explanation, and the most probable, is that it is merely an ordinary picture of Virgin and Child with the donors in adoration, and it is splendid enough in its simplicity without the need of any refined subtleties added to it by Teutonic sentimentalists.

The picture popularly known as *The Ambassadors*, formerly in the collection of the Earl of Radnor at Longford Castle, was purchased for the nation in 1890. Until that year the left-hand figure was always supposed to represent Sir Thomas Wyatt, poet and diplomatist, and his companion some unknown friend and fellow Ambassador, who, Dr. Woltmann suggested, was John Leland. When the picture was first exhibited in the National Gallery many suggestions were made as to their real identity, the most important being that of Mr. W. F. Dickes, who wrote several long articles to prove that they were the German Counts Palatine Otto Henry and his brother Philip, and that the picture represented "The Nuremberg Treaty of Religious Freedom between the Catholics and Protestants." Happily, the matter was settled in 1895 by Miss Mary F. S. Hervey, who discovered documentary evidence of so exact a kind that no doubt remains that the portraits are those of Jean de Dinteville, seigneur de Polizy, bailly de Troyes, and a knight of the French Order of St. Michael, and his friend, George de Selve, Bishop of Lavaur. Mr. Dickes, however, has recently returned to the charge (1901), doubts the evidence, and still pins his faith to his Counts Palatine.

Dinteville came here as French Ambassador more than once, and was in London in that capacity from February to November, 1533, the year in which the picture was painted, and during that time De Selve paid him a visit. George de Selve was appointed to the see of Lavaur in 1526, when only eighteen, but was not consecrated Bishop until 1534, and so in the picture is not shown in episcopal dress. He was one of six brothers, nearly all of whom gained distinction as Ambassadors. He himself served as Ambassador on a number of occasions, and his piety, his profound learning, and his keen interest in all intellectual pursuits, as Miss Hervey tells us in her exhaustive study of these two men and their picture, made him one of the most remarkable men of his day.

The two men stand on each side of a high, two-shelved table. Dinteville, on the left, is gorgeously dressed in a doublet of rose satin, with a black jacket and surcoat lined with ermine. His dark hair is cut straight across his forehead. De Selve, on the right, is clad in a long brocaded gown of chocolate colour, lined with brown fur. His hair and beard are also dark. Both shelves of the table are covered with a number of books, mathematical, musical, and other instruments, including a celestial and a terrestrial globe, sundial, lute, flutes, and other emblems of the pursuits in which they were interested. The curious object in the foreground is merely a distorted skull, which, when looked at from the side, assumes its proper proportions—a kind of optical puzzle, which had some vogue in the sixteenth century. The pattern of the pavement of coloured marbles was copied by the artist from the one in the Sanctuary of Westminster Abbey.

The many details of the picture have been painted with Holbein's usual accuracy and perfection. The faces of the two men are finely and delicately modelled, though their character is not quite so subtly expressed as in such a portrait as the *Duchess of Milan*. The dark, penetrating eyes and well-chiselled mouth of Dinteville give vitality to his intellectual face. De Selve is grave in contrast, with dark eyebrows and a more pallid complexion, and his countenance has less expression than is to be found in the other. The nobility of type of these two well-born, intellectual men is, however, admirably depicted by Holbein in a picture which is splendid both in colour and in treatment.

Holbein seems to have painted Erasmus three or four times, and as the originals were multiplied by copyists during the artist's life, there are still a large number of portraits of the great scholar in existence, all to-day ascribed to our painter. At least two of them were sent to England by Erasmus as presents to Sir Thomas More and Archbishop Wareham, one of which was the picture now at Longford Castle, and the other the fine profile in the Louvre, which was formerly in Charles I.'s collection.

The Earl of Radnor's *Erasmus* is a masterly and lifelike portrait. It forms a companion picture to the portrait of Peter Ægidius, by Quentin Matsys, also at Longford. For a long time both pictures were thought to be by the latter painter, as in 1517 these two learned men commissioned Matsys to paint a double portrait of them, which was sent as a present to Sir Thomas More.

Erasmus is represented in his black doctor's robes, heavily trimmed with fur, and a black cap. His hands rest upon a book, bearing the inscription, partly in Greek and partly in Latin, "The Herculean labours of Erasmus of Rotterdam." A curtain is behind his head, and on the left a stone pillar carved with fine Renaissance design. On the right a number of books are placed upon

[*Longford Castle.*Gray photo.]
PORTRAIT OF ERASMUS.
[*By special permission of the Earl of Radnor.*]

a small shelf, and on one of the volumes is the date 1523, and a half-effaced Latin distich, in which Holbein's name can still be read. The philosopher, turned slightly to the left, is gazing in front of him, deep in thought.

Mr. Claude Phillips has admirably described this picture (*Art Journal*, April, 1897). He says: "Holbein has rarely painted with a more exquisite subtlety or a firmer grip of his subject than here. The modelling of the head and hands is perfect in its searching truth and fine balance, showing none of that exaggeration and hardness of facial detail which so often mars the pictorial and obscures the intellectual conceptions in the portraits of Albrecht Dürer. Bodily suffering and advancing age have a little extinguished physical energy, but yet the great scholar of Rotterdam appears here surely but undemonstratively portrayed in his true character. He was the chief representative of the broader humanism in the Reformation, the one man able to look calmly at the world as it was—able to weigh, to judge, but also to show toleration—that is, provided his own comfort and security were not thereby interfered with."

The Louvre example, showing Erasmus writing, in profile, is smaller and richer in colour than the Longford example, and even more searching in its rendering of truth and character.

The superb portrait of *Georg Gisze*, member of the Hanse League and the London Steelyard, painted in 1532, shortly after Holbein's return to England, and now in the Berlin Gallery, is finer in its colour and more delicate in the rendering of its details than any other of the Steelyard portraits done by the artist about this time. It is almost Flemish in the minuteness and care of its finish and its clear colour, and seems to have had unusual pains bestowed upon it, perhaps as a kind of show-piece to tempt other sitters.

The young merchant is shown in his office, behind a table covered with a cloth of Eastern design, with the various objects that he requires in his business scattered in front of him and about the room. Among them is a graceful Venetian glass holding carnations. Papers and letters are fastened to the walls, one of which he is just opening, upon which can be read the address: "To the honourable Georg Gisze, my brother, in London, England." On the wall hangs a paper with his motto: "Nulla sine merore voluptas." He has fair hair, and is dressed in red, with black cap and overcoat, and a white shirt with a collar of Spanish work. All the accessories, whether of silk, or linen, or gold, or steel, or glass, are painted with a fidelity to nature never excelled by the Dutchmen or Flemings of the following century, who devoted their whole career to the rendering of still-life. In Holbein's work, however, this elaboration of detail is soon forgotten in the fascination which the vivid representation of the sitter's personality produces in the spectator and the power displayed by the artist in seizing the essentials of a character.

GEORG GISZE, MERCHANT OF THE STEELYARD.

Ruskin has described this portrait for us in words so eloquent and so glowing (*Cornhill Magazine*, March, 1860) that no excuse is needed for quoting a sentence or two here: "Every accessory is perfect with a fine perfection: the carnations in the glass vase by his side; the ball of gold, chased with blue enamel, suspended on the wall; the books, the steelyard, the papers on the table, the seal-ring with its quartered bearings—all intensely there, and there in beauty of which no one could have dreamed that even flowers or gold were capable, far less parchment or steel. But every change of shade is felt, every rich and rubied line of petal followed, every subdued gleam in the soft blue of the enamel and bending of the gold touched with a hand whose patience of regard creates rather than paints. The jewel itself was not so precious as the rays of enduring light which form it, beneath that errorless hand. The man himself what he was—not more; but to all conceivable proof of sight, in all aspect of life or thought—not less.

He sits alone in his accustomed room, his common work laid out before him; he is conscious of no presence, assumes no dignity, bears no sudden or superficial look of care or interest, lives only as he lived—but for ever. It is inexhaustible. Every detail of it wins, retains, rewards the attention with a continually increasing sense of wonderfulness. It is also wholly true. So far as it reaches, it contains the absolute facts of colour, form, and character, rendered with an unaccusable faithfulness."

According to Dr. Woltmann, Gisze belonged to a family residing in the neighbourhood of Basle, and even to-day, in the small adjacent town of Liestall, the name, in the form of Gysin, is to be seen over many houses. Even on the picture it is spelt in more ways than one. Miss Hervey considers it to be a variation of the surname Gueiss, one of the most distinguished in the annals of the Steelyard, and well known in Cologne. Georg Gisze was deputy Alderman of the Steelyard in 1533.

Shortly after the death of Queen Jane Seymour, in October, 1537, the Privy Council began to urge the King to marry again. The lady chosen was Christina, niece of the Emperor Charles V., daughter of the King of Denmark, and the young widow of Francesco Maria Sforza, last Duke of Milan, whom she married in 1534, when she was only eleven. He died in the following year, and in 1538 she was residing in Brussels at the Court of her aunt, the Regent of the Netherlands. Holbein, as "a man very excellent in taking phisanymies," was sent over to paint her portrait, and arrived there on March 10, accompanied by Sir Philip Hobby. A long letter to Cromwell from John Hutton, English Envoy to Flanders, gives us full details of this expedition. The lady's portrait had just been painted by some local artist, and despatched to Cromwell, on the eve of Holbein's arrival. When Hutton, however, saw the likeness which the latter produced in the space of three hours, which he considered "very perffight," he sent a messenger in haste to stay the delivery of the other, telling Cromwell that it was but "sloberid" in comparison. Holbein probably made one of his usual black-and-white crayon studies touched with colour, and from this, after his return to London, painted the full-length portrait belonging to the Duke of Norfolk, which he has lent so generously for a number of years to the National Gallery.

Christina stands, almost the size of life, facing the spectator, dressed in "mourning aparel after the manner of Italy"—a black satin gown, and over it a long black cloak lined with yellow sable. A black hood covers her hair and part of her forehead, and a ruby ring is her only ornament. You cannot call her very beautiful, but her expression is fascinating in the highest degree. It is painted with the utmost simplicity and directness, and yet is stamped with real grandeur of style in every delicate stroke of the brush. Her slender form ("She is of taller stature than either of us," wrote the Ambassadors Wriothesley and Vaughan) is admirably rendered, and Holbein, in the spirit of a true artist, has chosen to depict her in all the severity of her widow's weeds, rather than in the bravery of the Brussels court lady, thus giving an added effect to her sweet childish countenance, which is modelled in the most masterly fashion. Her dark eyes, from under fair eyebrows, seem to admit one to her most secret thoughts, and the red lips are full of expression. The flesh tints are unusually transparent, and a faint rosy glow of health just flushes her cheeks. "She is not so white as the late Queen," says Hutton, "but she hath a singular good countenance, and when she chanceth to smile there appeareth two pits in her cheeks and one in her chin, the which becomith her excellently well. She is higher than the Regent, a goodly personage of body and competent of beauty, of favour excellent, soft of speech, and very gentle in countenance." It is an exquisite portrait, and one of the most precious in the country.

For some reason, probably the Papal excommunication of Henry, the Emperor suddenly became hostile to this alliance, and the negotiations were broken off. She herself seems to have been not unwilling to become an English Queen. Sir Thomas Wyatt reported that she was somewhat flighty, but Hutton, on the other hand, mentions "her honest countenance, and the few words she wisely spoke." The popular tradition runs that she sent a respectfully sarcastic refusal to Henry, saying that "she had but one head; if she had two, one of them should be at His Majesty's service." She married Francis, Duke of Lorraine and Bar, in 1541.

One of the best of Holbein's portraits of English commoners is that of *Robert Cheseman* in the Hague Gallery, which was formerly in the royal collections of England. With his usual directness and faultless mastery of handling, he has given us here another example of exact portraiture, illuminated by a deep insight into

[*The Hague.* sHanfstängl photo.]
ROBERT CHESEMAN WITH HIS FALCON.

character. Cheseman, who is forty-eight, wears a silk doublet of purplish-red, with the customary black overcoat trimmed with fur. His curly hair is beginning to turn gray. He holds a hooded hawk on his gloved left hand, and strokes its feathers with his right. The bird is splendidly painted, and the keen, piercing eyes and clean-cut face of its master are wonderfully rendered. Sir Joshua Reynolds, who noted it during his travels in Holland, speaks of it as "admirable for its truth and precision, and extremely well coloured."

This picture is called erroneously in all the books "Henry VIII.'s Falconer," but he was a person of much more importance. Robert Cheseman, of Dormanswell, near Norwood, in Middlesex, and Northcote, in Essex, was a man of wealth, and one of the leading commoners of his county. He was born in 1485, son and heir of Edward Cheseman, Cofferer and Keeper of the Wardrobe to Henry VII., and succeeded to the family estates in 1517. He was made a Justice of the Peace for Middlesex in 1528, and during his life served on a number of commissions for collecting tithes, subsidies, and so on. In 1530 he was one of the commissioners on an inquiry into the possessions of Thomas Wolsey after he was attainted, and was on the Grand Jury at the trials of Sir Geoffrey Pole and others (1538), and Thomas Culpeper and Francis Dereham for treason (1541). He was one of the gentlemen selected to welcome Anne of Cleves when she first landed in England, and was, in fact, one of some half-dozen men of position who represented Middlesex on such public occasions. In 1536 he supplied thirty men for the army against the Northern rebels, so that he must have been a man of substance. He married Alice, daughter of Henry Dacres, of Mayfield, Staffordshire, a Merchant Tailor and Alderman of London. These curtailed biographical notes are inserted here, as they have not been previously published.

A small work of great beauty in Hampton Court Palace, representing *Mary Magdalen at the Sepulchre*, sometimes called *Noli Me Tangere*, is of unusual value to English students, as being the only sacred painting by Holbein now in this country. It has darkened greatly with age, and has suffered other damage, but is considered by most judges to be an undoubted original by the master, although Dr. Woltmann attributed it to Bartholomew Bruyn, of Cologne.

Both in treatment and in feeling this picture is very similar to the altar-piece of the Passion, in eight compartments, in the Basle Museum, and must have been painted about the same time, between 1520 and 1527. In sentiment it is one of the most poetical of Holbein's compositions, and an admirable example of his rendering of light and shade in his first Basle period. "The early morning when it was yet dark" is most successfully suggested in the painting of the landscape background. Dawn is just breaking over the sky and distant Calvary, while the foreground is still in darkness, except for the light which radiates from the open sepulchre, where

[*Hampton Court.* Hanfstängl photo.]
MARY MAGDALEN AT THE SEPULCHRE.
(*Also called* Noli Me Tangere.)

the two angels can be seen seated at the head and the foot of the empty grave. Mary, who holds a cup of spikenard in her left hand, has turned round hastily in eager surprise, and stretches out her right hand towards the Saviour. Our Lord draws back from her, saying, "Touch Me not!" The dramatic action of the two figures is most expressive. In the background the two disciples, who have been before her at the sepulchre, are seen hastening away. Peter, still dubious as to the truth of the Resurrection, is talking eagerly and with animated gestures as he expresses his doubts; but John, who "saw and believed," turns back his head in reproach at a comrade who can doubt even for a moment. The composition, as a whole, is marked by a simple but impressive dignity.

It seems almost certain that the first portrait painted by Holbein in England was that of *Sir Thomas More*. Mr. Huth's finished portrait, a half-length of the Chancellor, is dated 1527. There are two studies for More's head among the Windsor drawings almost identical. They are life-size, three-quarter face, looking to the right, with black cap and fur collar, done with black and red chalk. The drawing reproduced here is 16 inches high by 12 inches wide, and has been pricked for tracing. Holbein sketched the members of the More family on a larger scale than was usual with him, and all these drawings were preliminary studies for the large family group now lost, or hidden under the paint of some feebler contemporary artist in the Nostell Priory version of the picture. In these two drawings, in Mr. Huth's portrait, and in the large sketch for the family group now at Basle, Sir Thomas is represented in the same position, so that it is probable he only gave one sitting to the artist.

This drawing is masterly, and is a splendid example of how easily Holbein seized upon the leading characteristics of a face and with a few swift strokes fixed them for our admiration for ever. In his youth More had been handsome, and, according to Erasmus, was of a fair complexion, with dark-brown hair and gray eyes. His firmly-compressed lips and his penetrating glance give to his face a sternness which he seldom displayed, except in his detestation of heretics; but fine judgment and nobility of feeling, and that mental harmony which springs from inward peace, are the leading characteristics in his face as the artist has drawn it for us here. One can see at a glance that here was a man who would always be just in his dealings with others, and unchangeable in carrying out what he knew to be his duty—a student and a man of deep learning, and yet a man of affairs and of the world, trusted by his King and admired by his equals, and losing his head on the block through his invincible honesty. Erasmus well said of him: "He possesses that beautiful ease of mind, or, still better, that piety and prudence, with which he joyfully adapts himself to everything that comes, as though it were the best that could come."

[*Windsor Castle.* Colls photo.]
SIR THOMAS MORE, LORD HIGH CHANCELLOR.
[*From a drawing.*]

LIST OF THE ARTIST'S CHIEF WORKS IN PUBLIC GALLERIES

GREAT BRITAIN

WINDSOR CASTLE.

Sir Henry Guildford, Master of the Horse, 1527.

Hans of Antwerp and of the Steelyard, 1532.

Derich Born, of the Steelyard, 1533.

Thomas Howard, Third Duke of Norfolk, about 1540.

Christina of Denmark, Duchess of Milan, 1538.

A small panel, showing head and hands only, possibly an earlier study than the full-length belonging to the Duke of Norfolk.

HAMPTON COURT PALACE.

Elizabeth, Lady Vaux.

Small bust, partly repainted. There is a replica in Prague.

John Reskemeer, of Murthyn, Cornwall.

Mary Magdalen at the Sepulchre.

(See illustration)

NATIONAL GALLERY.

Jean de Dinteville and George de Selve ("The Ambassadors"), 1533.

(See illustration)

Christina of Denmark, Duchess of Milan, 1538

(See illustration)

BARBER SURGEONS' HALL.

Henry VIII. granting a Charter to the New Corporation of Barber Surgeons.

Holbein's last work, left unfinished.

NATIONAL GALLERY OF IRELAND.

Sir Henry Wyatt.

Replica of the picture in the Louvre, and formerly in the Magniac Collection.

AUSTRIA

VIENNA, IMPERIAL GALLERY.

Geryck (or Derich) Tybis of Duisburg and the Steelyard, 1533.

Queen Jane Seymour, about 1537.

A small half-length; there is a copy of it at Woburn Abbey.

Portrait of a Young Man, aged 28, 1541.

A very fine portrait, probably of an Englishman.

Dr. John Chamber, about 1541.

A small half-length of a very old man. Chamber's portrait in the Barber Surgeons' picture is one of the few heads in that work in which the hand of Holbein can now be traced.

Portrait of a Young Lady.

With an elaborate head-dress. Small half-length.

Portrait of an Englishman, aged 30, 1534.

Portrait of a Lady, aged 28, 1534.

Two small rounds on canvas; portraits of some English courtier and his wife, the man in a scarlet coat, with the letters H.R. embroidered in gold.

FRANCE

PARIS, LOUVRE.

William Wareham, Archbishop of Canterbury, 1527.

A replica of the portrait in Lambeth Palace.

Sir Henry Wyatt, 1527 or 1528.

The father of Sir Thomas Wyatt, the poet. Formerly called a portrait of Sir Thomas More. There is a replica of it in the National Gallery of Ireland.

Desiderius Erasmus, 1523.

Profile, turned to the left, writing. The oil-study for it is in the Basle Museum. Probably sent to England for More or Wareham, and exchanged by Charles I. with Louis XIII. for a *St. John Baptist*, by Leonardo.

Sir Richard Southwell, 1536.

A replica of the portrait in the Uffizi Gallery, but not so good. Another copy was exhibited by Mr. H. E. Chetwynd-Stapylton at South Kensington, 1866.

Nicholas Kratzer, of Munich, 1528.

Henry VIII.'s Royal Astronomer.

Anne of Cleves, 1539.

GERMANY

BERLIN, ROYAL GALLERY.

Georg Gisze, of the Steelyard, 1532.

(See illustration)

Portrait of a Young Man, aged 34, 1533.

Said to be a member of the Trelawney family, and perhaps a brother of the young man whose portrait, dated 1532, is in Count Schönborn's Collection, Vienna.

Portrait of a Man with a Long Beard, aged 54.

Formerly in the possession of Sir J. E. Millais, P.R.A. Painted about 1535 (?).

Portrait of a Young Man, aged 37, 1541.

Probably a Dutchman, of the Vos van Steenwijk family.

BRUNSWICK GALLERY.

Ambrosius (or Cyriacus?) Fallen, of the Steelyard, 1533.

Much repainted.

CARLSRUHE, KUNSTHALLE.

St. Ursula with the Arrows.

St. George and the Dragon.

Two panels, evidently parts of an altar-piece, one of them dated 1522. Some critics doubt the ascription, but they may have been designed by Holbein and completed by some other painter.

DARMSTADT, OLD PALACE.

The Meyer Madonna, about 1526.

(See illustration)

Portrait of a Young Man, 1515.

Dated and signed "H. H."

DRESDEN GALLERY.

Thomas Godsalve, of Norwich, and his son, Sir John Godsalve, 1528.

Two portraits on one panel. There is a fine drawing of Sir John in the Windsor collection.

Charles de Solier, Comte de Morette, of Piedmont, about 1534.

The Meyer Madonna.

A copy, with alterations, of the Darmstadt picture.

The Dresden Gallery also possesses copies of Erasmus and Henry VIII., after Holbein, and a picture, *The Death of Virginia*, said to be after some lost original.

FRANKFORT, STÄDEL INSTITUTE.

Simon George, of Cornwall.

FREIBURG-IM-BREISGAU, MINSTER.

The Nativity.

The Adoration of the Magi.

Altar-panels, painted for Hans Oberriedt, of Basle.

HANOVER, ROYAL GALLERY.

Edward VI. when Prince, 1538.

Half-length, life size. Other portraits of the Prince in the possession of the Duke of Northumberland (Syon House) and the Earl of Yarborough.

Philip Melancthon.

A small round, being a companion portrait to the small round of Erasmus at Basle, both probably painted about 1530.

MUNICH GALLERY.

Derich Born, of the Steelyard, about 1533.

A small oval, about 3 inches high, and seen slightly more in profile than the portrait of Born in Windsor Castle.

HOLLAND

THE HAGUE GALLERY.

Robert Cheseman, of Dormanswell, 1533.

(See illustration)

Portrait of a Young Man, aged 28, with a Falcon, 1541.

This splendid portrait is most likely that of an Englishman.

ITALY

There is only one undoubted example in Italy, and that is the fine portrait of Sir Richard Southwell in the Uffizi Gallery, Florence, of which there is a replica in the Louvre.

SPAIN

The single work by Holbein in Spain is a portrait of an old man, with an unusually large nose and a very ruddy face, which is in the Prado Gallery, Madrid. It appears to have been painted during Holbein's first visit to England.

SWITZERLAND

BASLE MUSEUM.

Virgin and Child, 1514.

This is the earliest known work of Holbein's, and was found in a village near Constance. Probably painted during his journey from Augsburg to Basle.

The Virgin Mary.

St. John the Evangelist.

Heads only. Two early works.

The Last Supper; The Scourging of Christ; The Prayer on the Mount of Olives; Christ taken Captive; Pilate washing his Hands.

Five Scenes from Christ's Passion, part of a series painted for some temporary purpose, such as the decoration of a church during Holy Week.

A Schoolmaster's Sign.

A board painted on both sides, representing the schoolmaster and his wife teaching pupils, and now split into two halves.

Jacob Meyer, Burgomaster of Basle, 1516.

Meyer's Second Wife, Dorothea Kannegiesser, 1516.

Adam and Eve, 1517.

Heads only; oil on paper.

Hans Herbster, 1517.

Until recently in Lord Northbrook's Collection, and now attributed in Basle to Ambrose Holbein.

The Last Supper.

The side portions are missing. Broken up and badly restored in Amerbach's time, and again restored and badly repainted at a later date.

Bonifacius Amerbach, 1519.

Portrait of Holbein.

In coloured crayons. It is not absolutely certain that this fine portrait represents the painter himself.

The Dead Christ in the Tomb, 1521.

Desiderius Erasmus, 1523.

In profile, writing. A study in oils for the portrait in the Louvre.

Johann Froben, the Printer.

This is a copy only.

The Passion of Christ, about 1524 or 1525.

An altar-piece of eight small panels in one frame.

Christ as the Man of Sorrows.

The Virgin as Mater Dolorosa.

Two small oil-paintings in monochrome as a diptych.

Two Doors of an Organ Case.

In monochrome. Formerly in Basle Minster. Figures of the Emperor Henry II. and his wife on one, and the Virgin and Child with Bishop Pantalus on the other.

Dorothea von Offenburg as "Lais Corinthiaca."

The same Lady as Venus, with Cupid.

Portrait of the Artist's Wife and Two Children, about 1528.

Desiderius Erasmus, 1530 (?).

A small roundel, from which the Parma portrait was probably painted. It is a companion work to the Melancthon at Hanover.

ZÜRICH, TOWN LIBRARY.

Painted Table, 1515.

Done for the wedding of Hans Bär, in Basle. Decorated with pictures of the amusing legend of St. Nobody, blamed in all households as the real cause of all accidents; and letters, a pair of spectacles, and other objects on the top, with the intention of deceiving the spectator.

MINIATURES AND DRAWINGS

Holbein undoubtedly painted a number of miniatures, but very few of these remain, although many are ascribed to him. Among the best are those of the two sons of the Duke of Suffolk, Henry and Charles Brandon, Catherine Howard, and Lady Audley, all at Windsor; others of Henry VIII. and Jane Seymour, belonging to the Seymour family; and a portrait of Holbein in the Wallace Collection.

The finest collections of drawings are those in Windsor Castle and the Basle and British Museums. Some good designs for jewellery will be found at Chatsworth.

CHRONOLOGY OF THE ARTIST'S LIFE

1497.	Born in Augsburg.
1514.	Left Augsburg. Date of his first known picture.
1515.	Settled in Basle with his brother Ambrose.
1517.	Living in Lucerne. Visited Altdorf.
1518.	Painted Hertenstein's house in Lucerne.
1519.	Back in Basle. Admitted to the Painters Guild.
1520.	Paid his fees as a burgher of Basle.
1521-22.	Decorated the interior of new Town Hall.
1526.	Painted The Meyer Madonna about this time. Left Basle, and reached England before the end of the year.
1528.	Returned to Basle in the summer, and bought a house.
1532.	Returned to England, and lived with the German colony in London.
1536.	In King Henry's service.
1537.	Painted the fresco in the Privy Chamber at Whitehall.
1538.	Went to Brussels to paint the Duchess of Milan. Made a second journey to "Upper Burgundy" in December, and spent a short time in Basle. The Dance of Death and Old Testament woodcuts published.
1539.	Went in August to Düren to paint Anne of Cleves.
1542.	Began the large picture in Barber Surgeons' Hall.
1543.	Died, probably of the plague, on some day between October 7 and November 29.

CHIEF BOOKS ON HOLBEIN

Blanc, Charles. Jean Holbein (dit le Jeune). Histoire des Peintres de toutes les Ecoles. 1860.

Cust, Lionel. Dictionary of National Biography.

His, Edouard. Dessins d'Ornements d'Hans Holbein. 1886.

Knackfuss, H. Holbein, translated by Campbell Dodgson, with 151 illustrations. 1899.

The latest and most accurate life, containing illustrations of a larger number of Holbein's portraits than in any other work.

Kugler. Handbook of Painting—German, Flemish, and Dutch Schools. Revised by Sir J. A. Crowe. Vol. I., pp. 198-218. 1898.

Law, Ernest. Holbein's Pictures at Windsor Castle. 1901.

Mantz, Paul. Hans Holbein, folio, Paris. 1879.

The best illustrated book on the artist, containing reproductions of the whole of the *Dance of Death* and *Old Testament* woodcuts, and the marginal drawings to *The Praise of Folly*.

Rousseau, Jean. Hans Holbein. Bibliothèque d'Art Ancien. 1885.

Ruskin, John. Ariadne Florentina. Lecture V. "Design in the German Schools of Engraving (Holbein and Dürer)." 1872.

Ruskin, John. "Sir Joshua and Holbein." *Cornhill Magazine*, March, 1860.

Woltmann, Alfred. Holbein und seine Zeit. Second Edition, 2 vols. 1874-76.

This is the leading work on Holbein.

Woltmann, Alfred. Holbein and his Time. Translation of the first edition by F. E. Bunnett, with 60 illustrations. 1872.

Wornum, R. N. Some Account of the Life and Work of Hans Holbein. 1867.

Wornum, R. N. Hans Holbein and the Meier Madonna. Arundel Society. 1871.